Everything You Need to Know About

SMOKING

Teenagers sometimes start to smoke because they think it will make them look "cool."

Everything You Need to Know About

SMOKING

Elizabeth Keyishian

Series Editor: Evan Stark, Ph.D.

THE ROSEN PUBLISHING GROUP, INC.
NEW YORK

Published in 1989, 1993, 1995 by The Rosen Publishing Group, Inc.
29 East 21st Street, New York, NY 10010

Revised Edition 1995
Copyright © 1989, 1993, 1995 by The Rosen Publishing Group, Inc.

Manufactured in the United States of America.

Library of Congress Cataloging-in-Publication Data

Keyishian, Elizabeth
    Everything you need to know about smoking/Elizabeth Keyishian
    (The need to know library)
    Includes bibliographical references and index.
    Summary: Discusses the dangerous effects of smoking. Why people
start, why it's so hard to quit, and how to stop smoking.
    ISBN 0-8239-2119-0
    1. Tobacco habit—Juvenile literature. 2. Smoking—Juvenile literature.
3. Youth—Tobacco use—Juvenile literature. [1. Smoking.]
I. Title. II. Title: Smoking. III. Series.
HV5745.K48   1989
813.85—dc20   89-10256
                                                      CIP
                                                      AC

Contents

Introduction

This book is called *Everything You Need to Know About Smoking*. It was written because there are so many things you do need to know about smoking, things that cigarette companies do not want you to know. Since many adult Americans have gotten smart and quit smoking—more than 40 million— the cigarette industry is targeting more young people like you to start where those who have quit left off.

They do this through clever advertising campaigns that target teens. Smoking seems glamorous when ads show young, fun couples or cartoon characters enjoying cigarettes. The three brands of cigarettes that use these types of ads are also the most popular brands among young smokers, pulling in 86 percent of the teenage market. Cigarette advertising has, unfortunately, been successful in encouraging young people to start smoking. This helps the companies while harming the health and shortening the lives of teenagers who become addicted to nicotine, the drug in tobacco smoke, before knowing the risks involved.

It is incredibly difficult to quit smoking once you

start, as any smoker will tell you. Nicotine, like heroin or cocaine, is an addictive drug. Although 40 million American smokers have quit, 50 million still smoke. Most people who smoke would like to quit but cannot. And many people who do manage to quit go back to cigarettes, even after not smoking for over a year.

Because of new laws that prohibit smoking in public places, it is becoming more difficult to be a smoker in social situations. This is because the health of non-smokers can be damaged by the sidestream smoke produced by cigarettes. Most non-smokers want to protect their lungs and would rather not be around harmful cigarette smoke. One ad campaign jokes about this by showing smokers on the wing of an airplane. They are saying that their cigarettes are worth going outside for. Smoking is actually a terrible incon-venience for smokers because now there are so few places where people are allowed to smoke.

So smoking causes serious damage to human health and offends many non-smokers. Unfortunately, even with this knowledge out in the open, many people are still interested in smoking. This book explores some of the reasons you or somebody you know may want to start smoking and gives you the facts you need to make an informed decision. It is one of the most important choices you will make in your lifetime about caring for yourself and your body.

The first cigarette can make you feel sick.

Chapter 1

Why Even Start Smoking?

Many young people start smoking to try something new. The problem is that just trying it once can be the first step toward an addiction, even if the smoker does not realize it at first. The best way to avoid getting addicted is not to start. This can be difficult, since teenagers receive many pressures from friends and the media. But standing up to these pressures is much easier than standing up to nicotine dependence.

It is also easier than paying the high price of cigarettes, especially the taxes on them. When making your decision to start or not start smoking, ask yourself about your future. Do you want to save up to buy a car? Would you like to have children some day? Do you want to live a long, healthy life? These things will all be affected by your decision.

Reasons Why

Why would people want to do something that is dangerous for them and for others? Why would they want to start something that is so hard to stop?

Some studies suggest that people start to smoke because the people around them do it. If your mother or father smokes, you are more likely to start smoking. If a sister or brother has started smoking, or a close friend, you are more likely to try it. When you admire people, you want to be like them. If you love or admire people who smoke, it is more likely you will start to smoke.

Some young people start smoking because they think it makes them look grown-up. They think that imitating grown-ups is the same as being an adult. Young people smoke because they see older people smoke and want to be treated as an adult, too. It is against the law for TV to have ads for cigarettes, but movies often show people smoking. And movies are shown on TV, too. So young people see famous, glamorous people smoking, and then think that smoking is okay. Think about movies you have seen. Do they show tough guys or beautiful young women smoking cigarettes? Think what those movies may "say" to you.

Researchers say that most people start smoking because their family or friends smoke.

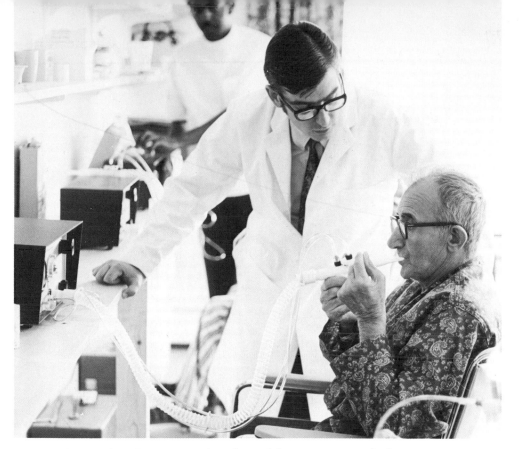

Lung disease is often a result of smoking over a period of time.

Many young people smoke because their friends do. Young people act alike because they feel better being part of a group than having to be alone. Feeling that you should do something because others do it is called *peer pressure*. (See Chapter 4: Everybody's Doing It. But Should You?) If one person in your group starts smoking, others may try it, too. And some of you might dislike it, but be afraid to tell the others. So all of you keep smoking. And if you continue to smoke, you may find it hard to stop. It will become a habit—a bad habit.

Some young girls start to smoke because they think that smoking will help them eat less.

Cigarette smoke contains *nicotine*, which is a drug. That means you may get *addicted* to smoking, and find it very hard to stop.

Think Again

Even if you thought smoking did help you to stay thin, you may not be considered attractive to others. Smoking gives you bad breath. It can stain your teeth. It makes your clothes smell bad. Even your hair will smell like tobacco if you smoke a lot.

You can tell that smoking is not good for you by the way your body reacts to it. The first time you smoke it usually makes you cough. You may choke or feel dizzy. You may even feel sick enough to throw up. Cigarette smoke contains *tar*. Tar stays in your lungs even though you blow the smoke back out through your nose or mouth. Tar in your lungs can cause cancer. Smoking can also cause heart disease and other serious health problems. Even if you *do* enjoy smoking, is the pleasure worth sacrificing your health or even your life?

You should think about all of these things when someone offers you a cigarette, or talks about how "cool" it is to smoke. Don't be afraid to say no. There are no good reasons to start to smoke. People will respect you for making your own decision.

Chapter 2

The Health Risks

We already know that smoking can lead to heart disease and lung cancer. But recently, a study was done that determined a link between cigarette smoking and colon cancer. If you start smoking when you are young, the increased risk of colon cancer stays with you even after you quit. In other words, it can cause permanent damage.

This is only one of the many discoveries scientists keep making about the negative effects of smoking on the human body. It may not seem important now, but you will be taking care of your body for a long time. Why not get a head start?

To understand how terrible smoking is for you, look at what each cigarette contains:

○ Nicotine—a habit-forming drug.
○ Black tars that stick to the lining of your lungs and make it hard to breathe.
○ Carbon monoxide and chemicals that poison your lungs.

Every drag on a cigarette leaves those things in your lungs.

Nicotine speeds up your heart. It makes your nerves shaky. In large doses, it is poisonous. You quickly become addicted to it.

The tars coat the inside of your lungs and make it hard to breathe. Your heart has to work harder. It is not getting enough oxygen from your stuffed-up lungs.

Carbon monoxide prevents oxygen from getting to your heart. That can cause heart disease.

How does smoking affect your body? Your body is like a sensitive machine. Its parts work together to keep you healthy. When you smoke, you damage many parts of the machine. That makes it break down. Soon, the machine stops working.

You breathe all day long. We take about 600 million breaths during our lifetime. When was the last time you said: "Wow. I'm breathing."

Smoking cuts down lung power. It becomes difficult to breathe while running or walking.

Probably never. You have too many other things to think about. You only think about breathing when it hurts to breathe.

When you smoke, you make breathing more difficult. Try running up a flight of stairs. You might find yourself breathing very heavily and your heart racing.

There are pictures that can show you what happens to your lungs and heart when you smoke. Surgeons who operate on smokers say that the lungs are black from tar.

Lungs bring oxygen into the body and pump carbon dioxide out. The lungs are made of tubes called *bronchi*. The tubes lead into tiny balloon-like sacs. In the tubes, tiny hairs (called *cilia*) brush mucus out of the airways.

Nicotine—the drug in the tobacco—paralyzes your cilia. The cilia can't push the mucus out of the way. Your airways get clogged. Tars and chemicals settle in the airways and the cilia die. The smoker has to cough to get the mucus out of the lungs. That's "smoker's cough." It sounds like someone choking and wheezing.

The bronchi (those tubes in your lungs) get sore with all that coughing. The smoker then develops "chronic bronchitis." It becomes more painful and difficult to breathe.

People with bronchitis often develop *emphysema*, a disease that makes it hard to breathe. Many of them have to use a wheelchair. Simple movements—like walking and breathing—are like climbing Mount Everest. Some people with emphysema are easy to spot. They have to wheel around a little cart of oxygen wherever they go.

People who smoke for a long time may also get cancer. The chemicals and tars in cigarettes make the body cells grow out of control. They form lumps—tumors—in the lungs. The cancerous lumps block breathing.

Smoking is also very hard on the heart. The lungs, heart, and blood vessels all work together. When you smoke, you breathe in nicotine and carbon monoxide. The nicotine and carbon monoxide make the blood vessels smaller. Less oxygen gets to the heart, so the heart has to work harder. Heart disease causes heart attacks.

There is *one* piece of good news. As soon as you stop smoking, your body begins to repair itself. The sooner you stop smoking, the less damage you'll do to your body.

Special Health Risks for Women

Smoking is dangerous for everybody. But there are special health risks for women.

Girls aged 14 to 17 are smoking more and more, even though there are health risks. That may be because of cigarette advertising. It may also be because they think that cigarettes keep weight down.

Lung cancer has replaced breast cancer as the leading killer disease of women. If you smoke and take birth control pills, you are TEN TIMES MORE LIKELY than average to have a heart attack or stroke. Smoking increases the risk of heart attack for young women more than any other factor. You don't have to be old to have a heart attack.

Remember the warning label: "Smoking by pregnant women may result in fetal injury, premature birth, and low birth weight."

Why should you worry about that now? It may not seem important to you yet. But once you start smoking, it is very, very hard to quit. When you become a mother, you may still be smoking.

Babies of mothers who smoke have twice the risk of having Sudden Infant Death syndrome. This kills babies, suddenly, in their sleep. Also, the babies of smokers have twice as many lung illnesses—like bronchitis and pneumonia.

Chapter 2: Summary

○ The earlier you start smoking, the earlier you can die from it.

○ Cigarettes contain nicotine, tars, carbon monoxide, chemicals. Nicotine is a habit-forming drug. Tars coat your lungs and make it difficult to breathe. Carbon monoxide is deadly for your heart.

A baby's health can be affected if its mother smokes.

○ Smoking causes lung diseases: chronic bronchitis and emphysema and lung cancer.
○ Smoking causes heart disease. Smoking gives people strokes and heart attacks.
○ The sooner you stop smoking, the less damage you will do to your body. But the longer you smoke, the higher your chances of getting lung or heart diseases.
○ There are special health risks for women who smoke. Lung cancer has replaced breast cancer as the leading cause of cancer death among women.
○ Women who smoke during pregnancy endanger their babies.

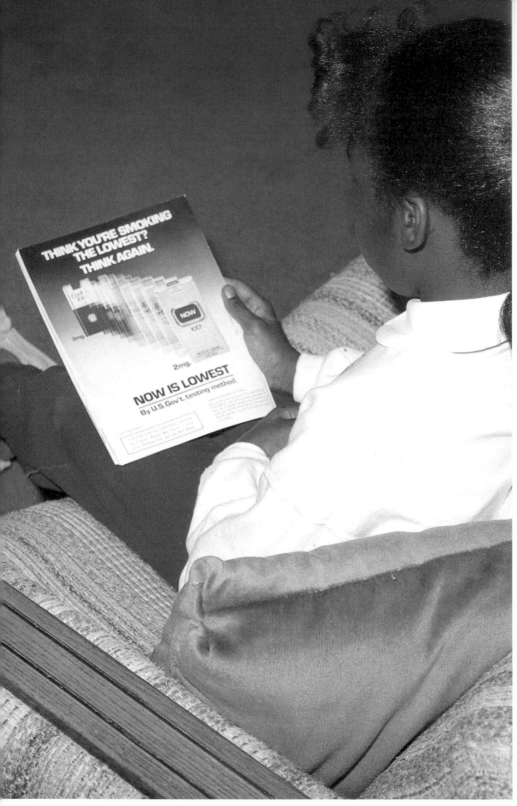

Cigarette ads always have a warning but they try to make smoking look safe and glamorous.

Chapter 3

What You See Is Not What You Get

Cigarette advertising has a hard job to do. Ads must make smoking look like something you will enjoy doing. They must make smoking look good enough to make you try it even though the same ad has a warning about smoking being harmful. The ads must have the warnings. That is the law. The law was passed so that everyone would know the dangers of smoking.

Older people who smoke don't need advertising to convince them. A lot of people who smoke would stop if they could, but they are "hooked." Smoking is a habit. You get used to it, and you miss it if you try to stop. And many people get addicted to the nicotine in tobacco smoke. Their bodies need it and they feel sick, or very nervous, if they do not smoke.

Older people who do not smoke will probably not be convinced by ads that smoking is a good thing. But tobacco companies and advertising executives think that they can make smoking look good to young people. That's why a lot of cigarette advertising is aimed at young people.

Cigarette ads show carefree couples having a good time. They make it look as if you will have fun because you smoke. They make you think that smoking will make you popular. That kind of advertising suggestion is called *association*. Linking something pleasant with a product makes people want to try the product.

Often the ads show couples outdoors together, or even show people playing sports. In real life, people who smoke a lot can have trouble breathing. Smoking makes it hard to play active sports. If you are on a team, the coach will tell you not to smoke.

Ads show people who are healthy, with glowing skin and brilliant white teeth. In truth, smoking stains your teeth. It makes your skin dull. It makes your hair smell bad.

Some people think that cigarette advertising should not be allowed. It is not allowed on TV. In the city of New York, cigarette advertising is not allowed on buses or subways any more.

It is against the law to sell cigarettes to minors (people younger than 18). But cigarette ads seem to be directed toward younger and younger kids. One cigarette company uses a cartoon character in its ads.

Sometimes the character is shown with a group of other "cool" characters. These ads appear on billboards and in store windows. They appear in magazines that kids read. One study showed that most fourth graders could more easily identify this cartoon character than a photo of the current president of the United States.

Cigarette companies sell, or give away with the purchase of cigarettes, T-shirts, caps, lighters, and other items. These items feature the name of their brand of cigarettes. When you use these items, you are giving the company *free advertising*. You become a walking cigarette ad!

A Different Kind of Advertising

There is another side to more recent cigarette advertising. Health-related groups like the American Cancer Society and the Heart Association have ads, too. Their ads stress the dangers of smoking. At first the advertising companies tried to block these kinds of ads. They threatened not to buy space from companies that sold space to anti-smoking ads.

But the message about the dangers of smoking is very important. The cigarette companies spend over a billion dollars a year to convince people that smoking is not bad for them. Now there is something being done to let people know the truth about smoking.

Friends will respect your wish not to smoke.

Chapter 4

It's Your Choice

As individuals, it is up to us to make our own decisions. We decide for ourselves what to do with our lives and with our bodies. That includes deciding what goes into our bodies.

It is important for us to make these choices, not to let others make them for us. If a friend offers you a cigarette, think before you accept it. Think carefully about everything you've learned about smoking. Are you ready to start an addiction that will put your health permanently at risk?

If not, there are ways to say no without offending your friends. If they are truly your friends, they will respect your decision. This is how the situation might go:

You are walking after school with Janelle, Lamont, and Greg, who pulls out a pack of cigarettes.

Greg: Anybody want one?

Janelle: God, do I need it.

Lamont: Me, too. You look like you could use one, too.

You: No, thanks, tryin' to cut down.

Janelle: Cut down? You've never even smoked.

You: I know. I don't really like cigarettes.

Greg: How do you know unless you try one? Here.

You: You guys, I really don't want to.

Lamont: Why not? It's no big deal.

You: Well, I don't know. For me, breathing is kind of a big deal.

Greg: Oh, please. We're breathing. Besides, one won't hurt you.

You: Yeah, but you know me. I'll smoke one, then I'll want another, and another, and another, and soon I'll be...

Janelle: Like us? Please, don't sink to our level.

You: No, it's not like that. You know I don't care if you smoke. It doesn't make me think any less of you guys. You're still the only people in our class as cool as me.

Lamont: (Laughing) Oh, thank you so much.

You: Well, almost as cool. Anyway, I just don't know if I'm ready yet. Maybe some day, but not now.

Greg: I just don't get what the big deal is. What's to be ready for?

Cigarettes are expensive. Saving some extra money can be a good reason not to smoke.

You: Well, they shorten your life. Everybody knows that, and I'm just not looking forward to death, you know? Anything that can prolong my life, I'm all for it. Plus, what if I want to have children?

Janelle: What do you mean?

You: Well, if I'm still smoking when I'm pregnant, it could hurt the baby.

Lamont: You're pregnant?

You: Shut up. Smoking when you're pregnant can even make your baby die before it's ever born.

Janelle: That would be so horrible. So incredibly horrible.

(Pause)

You: Well, on that cheery note, anyone for ice cream?

Chances are, if you keep your sense of humor and assure your friends that you are not judging them, they will respect your wishes without giving you much of a hassle. Just handle the situation tactfully but firmly, and they will probably not push you to smoke again. This will take a great deal of pressure off of you. And you will feel better about yourself when it is over.

Chapter 5

Smoking Is Drug Addiction

Every day we hear about the horrors of drug addiction. We read in the news about people overdosing on heroin or killing somebody to get money for crack. These are extreme cases of addiction, and most of us would not put smoking in that same category.

Like alcohol, nicotine is a legal drug. But that does not make it any less a drug. It may not have the immediate drastic effects of heroin or crack, but like those drugs, it is addictive. Smokers crave nicotine. They continue to smoke even though they know it is harming them. And they often go through withdrawal and relapse after quitting. These things characterize drug addiction.

A person addicted to cigarettes needs to light up first thing in the morning.

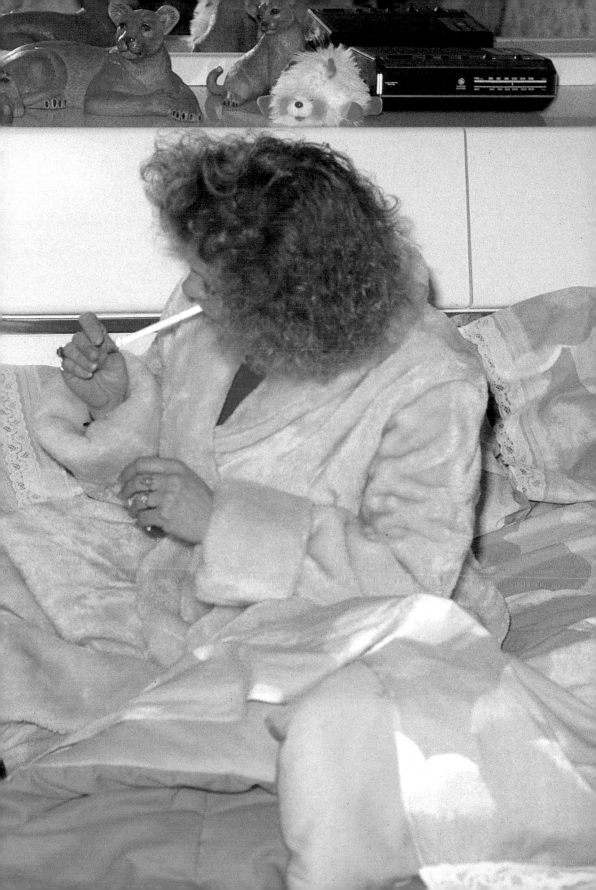

Smoking can give you a quick spurt of energy, but it does not last long.

When the nicotine level in the bloodstream gets low, the body signals the mind: "Smoke a cigarette. I need nicotine."

As soon as the smoker lights up, the nicotine is drawn into the lungs. It is quickly absorbed into the blood. The body's nicotine craving is satisfied—for a while.

Nicotine is a sneaky drug. When you first start smoking you find that smoking gives you a little burst of energy. That's the nicotine speeding up your heart.

But after a while you notice that you feel tired between cigarettes. That happens when the nicotine level gets low. The tired feeling is your body's way of telling you that it wants nicotine.

The smoker is like a prisoner on a seesaw. When you're "down" on the seesaw, your body feels "withdrawal." That's what makes you feel tired and sluggish. Your body wants its dose of nicotine.

So you smoke a cigarette.

Now you're "up" on the seesaw. Nicotine speeds up the heart. It gives you a "rush." It stimulates the *adrenal* gland. That's the gland that makes *adrenaline*—the stuff that pumps through your veins when you're excited or nervous.

That's what creates that seesaw feeling. The nicotine gives you a rush. But when the nicotine level goes down, you feel the withdrawal symptoms. So, although some people smoke to wake themselves up, they end up being more tired.

Chapter 5: Summary

○ When you smoke, your body becomes addicted to nicotine.
○ It is very easy to become addicted to nicotine.
○ Nicotine addiction makes you feel like a prisoner on a seesaw.

Many people think that smoking helps them to eat less.

Chapter **6**

Why Smoking Is Hard to Give Up

The addiction to nicotine is one BIG reason why it's hard to quit smoking. But it's not the *only* reason. If you've been smoking for a while, smoking becomes a habit.

Why is smoking so hard to give up? These four stories might give you an idea:

Darnell: "Three years ago, you would not have recognized me. I had a horrible weight problem. I weighed three hundred pounds until I started smoking. I don't know if I lost weight because I started smoking, but they happened at the same time. Anyway, I really would like to quit because I'm developing this annoying cough. I may be thin, but my teeth and fingers look really gross. The thing is, I'm kind of afraid to quit because I

35

hear you gain weight as soon as you stop smoking. The
last thing I want to do is put all that weight on again."

Darnell thinks that smoking keeps him thin.
Actually, smoking causes problems with your lungs
that prevent you from exercising. Darnell should
consider quitting smoking and starting a regular
workout and diet. These things are invigorating and
stimulating and keep you looking great. They are
much better ways to keep weight off than cigarettes,
with all their negative side effects. A jog in the sun-
shine can give you a rush similar to that of a cigarette.

Patsy: "I've been smoking for so long, it's become an
automatic reflex. When I light up, I'm not really
thinking about it. Usually I don't even realize I'm
holding a cigarette. Sometimes when I go out dancing, I
burn people without noticing. That is, until they start
screaming at me. Last week, I was sitting at my best
friend's dining-room table, smoking as usual, and I
must have nodded off. When she woke me, she was
freaking out because her mother's expensive tablecloth
was on fire. I was quite angry with myself."

One of the hardest things about quitting is that
smoking becomes an unconscious habit. It is never
easy to stop yourself from doing something that you
barely realize you are doing. It would be like trying
to quit eating, or brushing your teeth. That is how
Patsy feels about smoking.
Some people have "signals" to smoke. For

example, they may automatically light a cigarette whenever they finish a meal. For them, eating a meal is a signal to smoke. When trying to kick the habit, it is important to watch for these signals as problem areas to concentrate on.

Maria: "I've never been very good in social situations. I'm very shy. Smoking helps me relax and be myself, especially if I'm with a group of people. I try to go to parties instead of dinners or dances, because those places don't allow smoking. I really would feel better if I could quit smoking, but if I did I'd have no social life at all!"

Maria uses smoking as a crutch. Instead of concentrating on overcoming her anxiety with people, she believes that she solves her problem by smoking. Actually, smoking just covers up her problem so that she does not have to deal with it. Smoking does not actually solve anything.

Mark: "For as long as I can remember, I've been a very unhappy person. Depression gets a hold on me sometimes and just doesn't let go. During those times, it seems like the only thing that gets me through is a cigarette. When everything just seems too terrible to deal with, smoking gives me that little lift I need. If I quit, I don't know how I'd get through."

Mark is chronically depressed. It may be genetic; maybe one of his parents or relatives is

prone to depression. People who are this unhappy
need special help, and quitting smoking is extra
difficult for them. Smoking seems to ease their
depression for a short time. And when they do
quit, they are likely to sink into a much more
severe state of despair.

Often the only way of resolving this situation is
through professional help. Sometimes anti-
depressant drugs combined with a nicotine patch
or gum can wean the patient off of cigarettes without
too much difficulty. If you or anybody you know has
this problem, see a counselor or teacher at school.

Sometimes the problem is not quite so severe.
People often smoke just to relieve stress that comes
from day-to-day life. Instead of smoking, try
exercise to relieve stress. Taking a nap or a walk
can also be effective, or just watch a good movie.

If you know that a stressful situation is coming
up, try to plan ahead. Give yourself a healthy way
to get rid of the stress.

Smoking in bed is very dangerous.

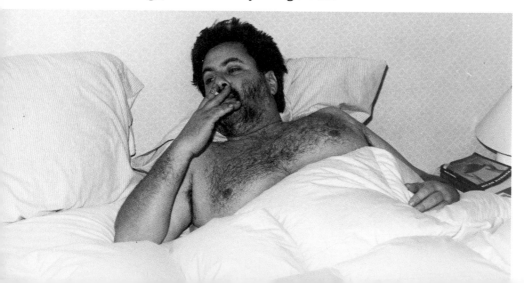

Smoking is not the way. It will end up causing stress, instead of helping it.

Chapter 6: Summary

° Smoking is hard to give up because it's a habit.

° Smoking is not a healthy way to keep your weight down. Many overweight people smoke. Exercise is a way to be lean and healthy.

° Smoking is something you might do without even thinking about it. Most smokers have "signals" that tell them when to light up. For example, a morning cup of coffee might be a signal to smoke.

° Many people smoke when they are under stress. School, family, work, even feeling tired can cause stress. There are healthy ways to deal with stress: exercise, nap, listen to music, take a walk.

Sports and smoking do not mix. Most smokers do not have enough energy to enjoy exercise.

Chapter 7

Good Reasons Not to Smoke

You may have heard this expression before: "Kissing a smoker is like licking an ashtray." Smoker's breath has also been called "zoo breath." Not only does a smoker's breath stink, but so do a smoker's hair and clothing. Smoking also leaves brown or yellow marks on teeth and fingers.

You might start smoking to be "in" with a certain group. But what about being friends with people who don't smoke? Many non-smokers think that smoking is disgusting. If you're a smoker, it could *limit* your social life.

Non-smokers don't like the smell of the smoke. They also don't like the fact that your cigarette smoke could hurt them. (See Chapter 8: Involuntary Smoking.) If you start smoking, you may actually lose more friends than you gain.

Smoking can limit your job options. Some places won't hire you if you smoke! And other companies put limits on where and when you can smoke at work.

The anti-smoking laws make it illegal to smoke in certain parts of restaurants. On short airplane flights, smoking is not permitted. Soon, smoking may be banned from all public places.

If you're still not convinced, think about this: Smoking is expensive. The cost of cigarettes is going up and up. Today, an average pack costs about $1.35. If you smoke a pack a day, that's $492.75 a year. With that much money, you could buy new clothes, go to seventy movies, or even pay for part of a sunny vacation.

Other costs include dry-cleaning bills. You need to spend extra money to get the cigarette smell out of your clothes.

Smoking also limits your sense of smell. And studies have shown that smoking gives you wrinkles and makes your skin look unhealthy.

Chapter 7: Summary

○ Smokers have stinky hair, breath, and clothes. Smoker's breath has been called "zoo breath."

Bad breath is not romantic! Many smokers use gum or mints to cover up cigarette breath.

- Smoking can limit your social life. Non-smokers don't want to be exposed to the health risks of smoking. Also, they don't like the stink of smoke. So non-smokers may avoid smokers.
- Smoking can limit your job options.
- Anti-smoking laws make it illegal to smoke in sections of restaurants and in some public places.
- Smoking is expensive.
- Smoking limits your sense of smell.
- Smoking gives you wrinkles and makes your skin look unhealthy.

Non-smokers are affected by the smoke around them.

Chapter 8

When Others Smoke

Let's say you don't smoke. Think about riding in a car or being in a closed room with a smoker. But the smoker's burning cigarette makes it hard for *you* to breathe.

New studies have shown that this smoke—from someone else's cigarette—can be harmful to *your* health. Non-smokers are very angry about this.

Most states in the United States have a law that protects non-smokers. It is illegal in those states to smoke in many public places, like elevators and some buildings. Some states require that restaurants have two sections: one for smokers, and one for non-smokers. It is also against the law to smoke cigarettes, or tobacco in any form, on airplanes. Many workplaces have also been declared "smoke-free zones."

What are non-smokers worried about?
There are two kinds of smoke that come from a
lighted cigarette:
  1) "mainstream" smoke
  2) "sidestream" smoke

Mainstream smoke is what the smoker inhales
into his or her lungs. Think of a smoker taking a
drag in slow motion. The smoke passes through
the filter of the cigarette. The filter traps some of
the chemicals and tars. Then the smoke enters the
lungs. The lungs filter out more of the harmful
substances. Then the smoker exhales.

Sidestream smoke is the smoke that goes directly
into the air from the tip of a burning cigarette.
This smoke does not pass through a filter. It
contains a lot more carbon monoxide, tars, and
nicotine than the mainstream smoke.

Sidestream smoke is what non-smokers breathe
when they are in a room with smokers. The carbon
monoxide makes them feel tired. It gives them
headaches. Studies have shown that non-smokers
who live with smokers die younger than people
who live in smoke-free houses.

A famous television writer died of lung cancer.
He had *never* smoked. His partner had smoked
more than two packs of cigarettes every day. The
two men had worked together for over 20 years.
How do you think the surviving partner felt about
what had happened? Would you want something
like that to happen to someone you care about?

The smoke from lit cigarettes in the ashtray can be harmful.

What does all this mean? The non-smoker who lives or works with smokers can get as sick from the smoke as smokers. Is that fair?

What do you think?

Chapter 8: Summary

○ The smoke from a cigarette can harm non-smokers too.

○ Mainstream smoke is what a smoker inhales. It is filtered by the smoker's lungs. More poisonous to the non-smoker is sidestream smoke. That smoke contains all the unfiltered poisons: tars, carbon monoxide, etc.

○ The non-smoker who lives or works with smokers can also get sick from smoke.

Talking with counselors and other teens can be helpful in making a decision about not smoking.

Chapter 9

Do You WANT to Smoke? Make Your Own Decision

Now you know more about smoking. You know how it affects your body, your appearance, and your health. You know more about why people start and why it's hard to stop.

Maybe you haven't started smoking, but you're thinking about it. Choosing whether or not to smoke is an important decision. This "test" will help you. If you're already a smoker, try this test. It may change your mind about smoking.

This is the "Smoker's Decision Test." It isn't like a school test. There are no right or wrong answers. This is a way to help you get a clearer idea of what's important to you. It will help you make the decision about smoking.

Check one box for each statement.

Part One: Reasons for Smoking

	Very Important	Not Important
1. Smoking can make you feel like part of the group.	☐	☐
2. Smoking can make you feel more mature and glamorous.	☐	☐
3. If you already smoke, you'd be giving up something that makes you feel good.	☐	☐
4. Smoking relaxes you.	☐	☐
5. You don't want to admit that it was a mistake to start smoking.	☐	☐
6. Quitting might cause you to gain weight.	☐	☐
7. You don't want to face the possibility that your smoking is out of control and you can't quit.	☐	☐

Most people find it easy to use the result of this test. They can see clearly how they feel about smoking.

Look at what you have checked. Look closely at what you have checked in the "Very Important" column.

Check one box for each statement.

Part Two: Reasons for Not Smoking

	Very Important	Not Important
1. Smoking can limit your social life.	☐	☐
2. Smoking is bad for your health. It can even kill you.	☐	☐
3. It is bad for the health of others around you.	☐	☐
4. It has special health risks for women.	☐	☐
5. It can limit job opportunities.	☐	☐
6. It reduces athletic ability.	☐	☐
7. It is an expensive habit.	☐	☐
8. It makes your breath, clothes, and hair smell bad.	☐	☐

Now write out your "Very Important" reasons for smoking and your "Very Important" reasons for not smoking. Compare them side by side.

Look at your reasons. DECIDE FOR YOURSELF if you are going to start. If you have already started, decide if you are going to continue or quit. Either way, make your own decision.

Setting a date is an important part of trying to stop smoking.

Chapter 10

How to Quit Smoking

If you are a smoker, you may have tried to quit. You may have found that it's very, very hard.

Now the good news! Nearly half of all living adults who ever smoked have quit. That's *millions* of people who have quit smoking. You can too. There is no guaranteed method. You have to find what's right for you. Here are some steps to follow to help you kick the habit.

1. Don't Leave Home Without It

Make a list of all the reasons why you want to quit. (I hate the way cigarettes smell. I want clean lungs.) *You* must decide why you want to quit. Is it the cost? The complaints from your boyfriend or girlfriend about the smoke?

Write down those reasons. Keep the list with you. Every day, pull out the list and remind yourself: This is why I'm quitting.

2. Set a Date

Choose a quitting date on the calendar. Don't change it. If you know you smoke most often at school or work, choose a weekend to quit. That will make the first one or two days easier.

Some people quit "cold turkey." That means they choose a day to quit, and they quit—completely.

Other people cut down first. That means that they smoke fewer cigarettes. Then they quit.

3. Cutting Down

The cutting down period should last only three weeks. Set your quitting date for three weeks later.

Here's how to cut down:

You probably smoke a certain number of cigarette without even thinking about it. Other cigarettes, like the ones you smoke after a meal or after a test, are more important to you. At those times you really *want* a cigarette.

The trick to cutting down is to decide which cigarettes are important to you—and smoke ONLY those cigarettes.

You can plan ahead of time. Carry a cigarette pack with the exact number of cigarettes you have decided to smoke that day. It might be just three or four.

Another way to cut down is to smoke only half a cigarette at a time. Or change to a brand of cigarettes you don't like.

Still another way to cut down is to delay having a cigarette when you want one. Instead of smoking when you want to, wait ten minutes. That way, you can think it over and decide if you *really* want that cigarette. You may find that after ten minutes you don't want the cigarette anymore.

Cutting down is great. But don't fool yourself. You may think that you have things under control. You may think you can quit anytime. That's not true. Most people who cut down soon return to their original number of cigarettes.

Limit the cutting-down period to three weeks. Set your quitting date!

4. Tell Everybody You're Quitting

Tell your family and friends about your plan to quit smoking. That will make it harder for you to back out of it. It will also let others know that you might be cranky and a little hard to live with for a few days.

5. Don't Change Your Eating Habits

Don't reach for a snack every time you want a cigarette. Chew gum. Exercise. If you snack, that might make you gain weight. People use weight gain as an excuse to start smoking again.

6. Reward Yourself

Find other things to do that are fun or make you happy. An easy choice is exercise. Exercise is good because you have to use your lungs and body. That reminds you of how important clean lungs are. Also, exercise makes you feel good.

Or take up a hobby—photography, music, skateboarding.

Go to the movies, the zoo, the beach, a concert. To pay for these activities, use the money you're not spending on cigarettes!

7. DON'T GIVE UP!

If you smoke a cigarette or even an entire pack, don't feel that you've failed. Pull out your list and remind yourself why you want to quit. If your reasons have changed, make a new list.

Watch for "smoke signals"—like a friend lighting up. Know that this is the time when you're most likely to smoke. Be strong. It will pay off.

Chapter 11

Finding Help

It is very hard to quit smoking. If you need help, don't be afraid to ask for it. There are many organizations that are ready to help.

The American Cancer Society has a program called "Smoking Cessation Clinics for High School Students." The program is made up of nine one-hour sessions. The Cancer Society trains someone from your school, the school nurse or a teacher. That person runs the clinic.

Check with your principal, school nurse, or guidance counselor to find out if your school offers this program. If the school doesn't have the program, you can help get one started. Look up

the American Cancer Society in your local
phone book. Or write to:

American Cancer Society
19 West 56th Street
New York, NY 10019

The American Lung Association and the
American Heart Association are two other
organizations that are ready to help. They each
have many stop-smoking programs. Write to:

American Lung Association
1740 Broadway
New York, NY 10019

American Heart Association
7272 Greenville Avenue
Dallas, TX 75231-4596

Quitting smoking is always a positive step. No
matter how long you have smoked, your body will
recover from at least some of the bad effects once
you stop.

If someone you know has tried to quit and
failed, maybe a doctor can help. Drugs are now
available to help those who can't seem to quit.
Some people have been helped by a chewing gum
that a doctor can prescribe. And some people
have been helped by wearing patches on their skin.
The patches release nicotine into the body. The
chewing gum also provides the body with nicotine.
These people cannot break their addiction to
nicotine. But at least their lungs—and the lungs of
those around them—are no longer in danger.

Glossary—*Explaining New Words*

addictive   Causing a person's body to depend on a chemical.

adrenal gland   Produces the hormone adrenaline. Adrenaline prepares the body for emergency action. It makes the heart work harder.

bronchi   Tubes in the lungs.

cancer   A disease that causes cells to grow abnormally and become tumors. These tumors spread and interfere with normal cell growth.

carbon dioxide   A gas that is breathed out of the body when exhaling.

carbon monoxide   A gas that is poisonous. It is one of the chemicals in cigarette smoke.

chronic bronchitis   A lung condition caused by smoking. It is marked by severe coughing and irritation of the lungs.

cilia   Tiny hairs in the bronchi that clear away mucus.

craving   A great desire or longing.

drag   A slang term for inhaling cigarette smoke.

emphysema   A severe lung disease.

glamorous   Full of excitement and romance.

heart disease   There are many different diseases, including heart attack, stroke, hardening of the arteries, and blood clots.

influence   To sway or affect.

mainstream smoke   What the smoker inhales.

mucus   A slippery secretion of the mucous membranes.

nicotine   A drug found in tobacco smoke that your body becomes addicted to.

passive smoking   Being affected by the smoking of others.

peer pressure   A feeling that you should do something because others do it, or want you to do it.

premature (birth)   Early, before fully ready.

sidestream smoke   The smoke that comes from the burning end of a cigarette.

stress   Tension or pressure.

tar   A sticky, black substance found in tobacco. It coats the lungs when smoke is inhaled.

withdrawal   Process of stopping the body's dependency on an addictive drug. Physical and mental effects an addict suffers after ceasing to take an addictive drug.

For Further Reading

Casey, Harry F. "A Sure Way to Stop Smoking."
   Reader's Digest (Canadian). September 1986,
   pages 71–74. This article gives a scary
   description of lung cancer.

Goode, Erika F. "A New Addictive Drug:
   Nicotine." *U.S. News & World Report*. May 30,
   1988, pages 63–64. This article discusses the
   effects of nicotine on the body.

Krogh, David. *Smoking, The Artificial Passion*. New
   York: W.H. Freeman & Co., 1991. This book
   for young people is a history of smoking, which
   includes a chapter on how to quit smoking.

Malanka, Phyllis A. "Why Do We Smoke?"
   Health. February, 1986, pages 32–35. This
   article discusses why people might start smoking.
   It also discusses specific health risks to smokers.

Robinson, Mary. *Giving It Up Mom*. New York:
   Houghton Mifflin, 1989. This book is fiction,
   but its message is real. Kids can help their
   parents to quit smoking.

Teltsch, Kathleen. "Keeping Teen-Agers
   Smokeless." *The New York Times*, August 18,
   1992, pages B1, B4. A town in New Jersey
   works hard to keep teens from smoking.

Index

About the Author

Elizabeth Keyishian is an Associate Editor for an award-winning children's science magazine. In addition to writing for young adults, she has published humorous essays (most recently in *Glamour* Magazine.) A graduate of Wesleyan University, Ms. Keyishian lives in New York City.

About the Editor

Evan Stark is a well-known sociologist, educator, and therapist as well as a popular lecturer on women's and children's health issues. Dr. Stark was the Henry Rutgers Fellow at Rutgers University, an associate at the Institution for Social and Policy Studies at Yale University, and a Fulbright Fellow at the University of Essex. He is the author of many publications in the field of family relations and is the father of four children.

Acknowledgments and Photo Credits

P. 11 H. Armstrong Roberts, Inc.; all other photos, Stuart Rabinowitz

Design/Production: Blackbirch Graphics, Inc.
Cover Photograph: Stuart Rabinowitz